How to Play the Fife for Beginners

The Ultimate Guide to Learning, Playing, and Becoming Proficient at the Instrument

© **Copyright 2023 - All rights reserved.**

The content contained within this book may not be reproduced, duplicated, or transmitted without direct written permission from the author or the publisher.

Under no circumstances will any blame or legal responsibility be held against the publisher, or author, for any damages, reparation, or monetary loss due to the information contained within this book, either directly or indirectly.

Legal Notice:

This book is copyright protected. It is only for personal use. You cannot amend, distribute, sell, use, quote, or paraphrase any part of the content within this book without the consent of the author or publisher.

Disclaimer Notice:

Please note the information contained within this document is for educational and entertainment purposes only. All effort has been executed to present accurate, up-to-date, reliable, and complete information. No warranties of any kind are declared or implied. Readers acknowledge that the author is not engaging in the rendering of legal, financial, medical, or professional advice. The content within this book has been derived from various sources. Please consult a licensed professional before attempting any techniques outlined in this book.

By reading this document, the reader agrees that under no circumstances is the author responsible for any losses, direct or indirect, that are incurred as a result of the use of the information contained within this document, including, but not limited to, errors, omissions, or inaccuracies.

Table of Contents

Introduction 1

Chapter 1: Get Acquainted with the Fife 3

Chapter 2: A Practical Dive into the
World of Fife 11

Chapter 3: Decoding the Complex
World of Fife Musical Notation 18

Chapter 4: The Secrets of Mastering
Proper Fingering Techniques...................................... 30

Chapter 5: Producing Your First Tones 37

Chapter 6: Basic Melodies and Exercises 45

Chapter 7: Exploring Different Musical
Styles and Level Up Fife Skills with Intermediate
Techniques and Genre Exploration 53

Chapter 8: Progressing as a Fife Player 58

Conclusion 63

References 66

Introduction

A close kin to the flute and piccolo, the fife is a remarkably diverse and enigmatic instrument. Yet, it remains a road less traveled and a challenge only embraced by the most resolute of souls.

When it comes to mastering the fife, you're on a solitary quest. The internet offers meager guidance, and the literary world overwhelmingly favors its woodwind cousins, the flute, sax, and piccolo. Only a scarcity of helpful guides are available. Even the dusty shelves of libraries may discourage you with tales of complexity and esoteric techniques. But here, in the pages of *"The Ultimate Guide to Learn Fife as a Beginner,"* you'll find the help. This book rises to the challenge, delivering not only information but a practical, easy-to-follow narrative, empowering you to embrace the mantle of a master fifer.

If you want to master this intriguing instrument, your journey begins here. They say that mastering the fife's embouchure is arduous, and coaxing the perfect tone is even more elusive. Yet, armed with the right tricks and techniques, guided by step-by-step instructions and comprehensive lessons in music theory and note mastery, your destination as a pro fifer becomes inevitable.

To the aspiring fifer: do not let preconceived notions deter you from your chosen path. Hold steadfast. This guide, tailored to the 6-hole fife, will be your trusty compass through the labyrinth of ultimate mastery. Within its pages, you'll uncover the secrets of the fife's ethereal high-pitched notes, a realm known solely to fifers. Prepare yourself for the ultimate journey toward becoming a true fifer, a challenging and profoundly rewarding journey.

Chapter 1: Get Acquainted with the Fife

The instruments in the woodwind family create a diverse range of high and low notes and sounds. Woodwind instruments like flutes, fifes, and piccolos have been some of the most essential members of orchestra ensembles and marching bands. One of the star members of the woodwind family appearing in the marching band ensemble is the fife. This instrument has as rich a history as the other members of the woodwind family. However, it is not talked about as much compared to its more popular counterparts, like flutes and piccolo.

This chapter goes into the humble beginnings of the fife, its origins, and how this instrument has evolved over the years.

Are you wondering why you need to know about the fife before picking up the instrument? Well, learning an instrument is about developing a connection with it spiritually, mentally, and physically. Your connection will improve how well you play the fife significantly. This chapter will help you unravel how this instrument has stood of time and remained significant in many cultures.

What Is a Fife?

Often, many aspiring musicians who aim to master this particular instrument seek clarification regarding the distinction between flutes and fifes. It is essential to comprehend what a fife truly is to gain a complete understanding of this instrument and enhance your ability to play it.

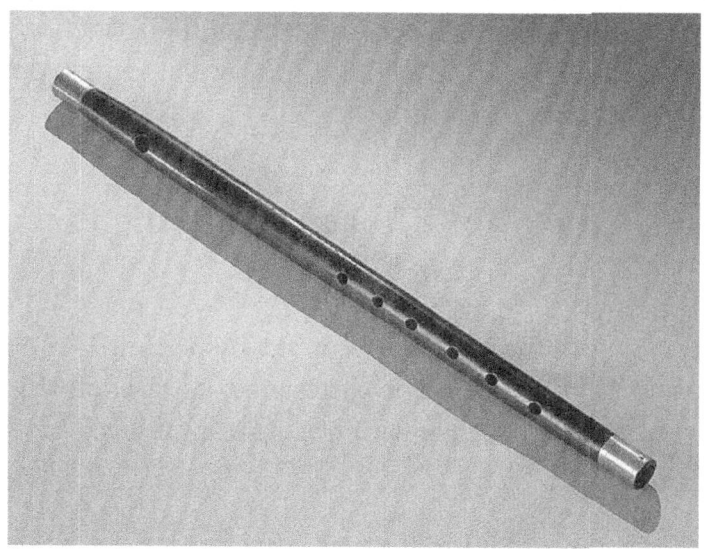

1. *The fife is a high-pitched woodwind instrument. Source: User Kevin Saff on en.wikipedia, Public domain, via Wikimedia Commons: https://commons.wikimedia.org/wiki/File:Fife-wooden,_civil_war_era.jpeg*

A fife is a slender, high-pitched woodwind instrument characterized by a transverse design and a narrow cylindrical body with six finger holes. However, modern variations can boast 10 or 11 finger holes. Its elongated and conical bore design signifies its propensity for producing sharp, resonant tones.

The term *"fife"* originates in the German word *"pfeife,"* which translates to *"pipe."* This mezzo-soprano member of the woodwind family produces piercing, loud notes, predominantly in the key of Bb. Playing it within an ensemble necessitates transposing the instrument.

The fife, preceding the flutes and piccolo's emergence, is an early, rudimentary instrument with a rich historical legacy explored in subsequent sections. However, as a novice fifer, it's imperative to grasp the fundamental distinctions and connections between the fife and other related instruments, specifically piccolos and flutes.

How Is the Fife Different from the Piccolo and Flute?

How do you differentiate between a whisper and a murmur? Or a pond from a lake? The differences and similarities are quite subtle, as is the case with fife, flute, and piccolo.

Fife vs. Flute

Among the two instruments, the fife has a simpler anatomy than the flute. It has a narrow bore to play in the second and third octaves. The flute has a broader bore to play the first and second octaves and, at times, the third.

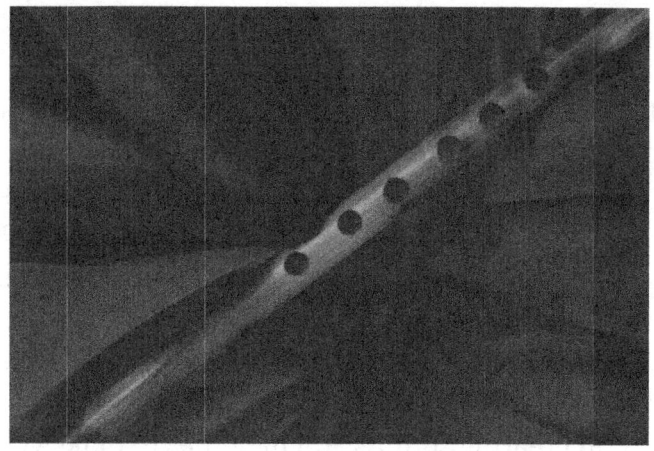

2. *A flute has a more complicated anatomy than a fife. Source: https://unsplash.com/photos/brown-flute-wfVREQs7KXQ?utm_content=creditShareLink&utm_medium=refe rral&utm_source=unsplash*

The flute is a more chromatic instrument with multiple tone holes to play in various keys. Whereas the fife plays in the B-flat key, the pitch and scale vary with the manufacturer.

Fife vs. Piccolo

The fife and piccolo are similar in size. Both are smaller than flutes and other woodwind instruments. However, that's where the similarities end.

One of the main distinctions between fife and piccolo is their anatomy. The fife is a one-piece organ with hollow tone holes, whereas a piccolo has two detachable pieces and comes with tone keys. Moreover, the fife has a longer length and smaller cylindrical bore, giving it a shrill sound but not as loud as a piccolo. When played side-by-side, you'll realize that the fife produces bright, open, and piercing sounds. The piccolo offers a shrill yet sweet, delicate sound.

The differences between the fife, flute, and piccolos are too subtle and minute to pick apart. However, they all sound distinct, with different pitch, tone, and timbre. While these three instruments are suitable for various music genres, each has a preference. For instance, flutes are fabulous when played in orchestras, choirs, jazz, and concert bands. Piccolos can be the perfect companion for solo performances, wind ensembles, chamber music, and orchestras. Similarly, no marching band and drum corps performance is complete without fife. Moreover, the drum and fife combination is one of the best at creating sounds and melodies to make your body feel alive.

Origins of the Fife

The fife isn't the most current or sought-after instrument in the modern music scene, like its counterpart, the flute. But does that mean the fife holds no significance or has no place in modern times? That's not entirely true. Interestingly, the fife antedates the flute regarding its origin and primitive nature. Furthermore, the fife had and still has, a significant place as an essential musical instrument in military bands, marching bands, and drum and corps performances.

Tracing the Roots of Fife through the Years

The fife's earliest records date back to ancient and prehistoric times. The most primitive form of this instrument was carved from the bones of animals like cave bears, vultures, and mammoths. While similar forms of these woodwind instruments can be traced back 50,000 years ago, these claims require more evidence. More accurate records and research put the origin of the fife around the 1300s in ancient Greece. The fife was also prominent throughout medieval Europe and Eastern European cultures.

Fife as a Military Instrument

During the 15th century, the Swiss and Germans used the fife in the infantry units. During the Revolutionary War, the British and American armies actively used it on the battleground to signal camp duties and time for battle. Throughout the colonial period in New England, the fife rose to even higher popularity alongside orchestral instruments like the cello, piano, and violin. More importantly, the fife's notoriety as a military instrument has remained consistent from its emergence to current times.

Are you wondering why the fife has stayed so relevant throughout its history as a military instrument? The answer is attributed to this instrument's impressive dynamics. Historical records show that it was valued for its shrill and loud tone, as it could be heard from a distance of three miles and even over artillery fire.

The Fife and Drums in Marching Performances

The legacy of the fife in marching bands has remained an unbroken tradition in Irish, Welsh, German, and English military units. However, no performance or ensemble is complete without including both the fife and drums. These two are constant partners in every military corps and marching performance, which poses the question, why? The fife has a relatively high frequency and pitch, making it an extremely hard instrument to be precise with. This instrument's loud dynamics and pitch make it extremely difficult to play in tune with others in the ensemble and achieve harmony. Hence, the fife pairs well with percussion instruments.

Fife as an Instrument for Folk Music

While the fife has a strong history in military settings, it was also used to belt out folk tunes. The fife in folk music really came to the fore in the 20th century. Since the fife dates back to medieval Europe, this instrument has been used to play folk music, Celtic, old-timey, and folk rock tunes. Not only in Eastern Europe, but the fife arrangement also had a strong presence in the U.S. colonial period, leaving traces and influences in Appalachian folk music. Additionally, its influence reached African and Brazilian music.

Development of the Modern Fife

The development of the modern fife is a fascinating journey through time, marked by several significant milestones. The fife's roots can be traced back to ancient civilizations as a signaling and ceremonial instrument. However, its evolution into the modern form was a gradual process that spanned centuries.

A key turning point in the development of the modern fife occurred during the Renaissance period. During this era, the instrument underwent significant changes in its design, including the addition of finger holes and improvements in its construction. These modifications allowed for a wider range of musical expression and versatility in the instrument's use. Its compact size and sharp, piercing tone made the fife popular in military bands and for signaling troops and leading them into battle.

The Baroque period further contributed to the fife's evolution. This era witnessed advancements in craftsmanship and bore design, which enhanced the instrument's tonal quality. Composers incorporated the fife into their compositions, giving rise to a repertoire specific to the instrument. It also gained prominence in courtly and chamber music, demonstrating its adaptability across various musical genres.

The 19th century saw further refinements in fife design, with the addition of more finger holes to extend its range. This period also witnessed the standardization of the fife in pitch and key, with the Bb fife becoming the most common variant. The instrument found its way into marching bands and continued to play a significant role in military settings.

The fife has retained its unique place in music in the modern era. It is often used in folk, traditional, and contemporary music thanks to its distinctive timbre and historical significance. The development of the modern fife is a testament to its enduring appeal, as it continues to captivate musicians and enthusiasts alike with its rich history and versatile sound.

Chapter 2: A Practical Dive into the World of Fife

Once you have developed a connection with the fife and understood its humble beginnings, the next step to becoming a master fifer is getting acquainted with the instrument. You have to understand how all the parts of the instrument come together in perfect harmony to produce a musical sound. This chapter is your first practical insight into the world of fife.

You will learn about the parts of the fife, its various types, and functions to understand how this instrument works. Once done, you'll want to rush to get your hands on a brand new or a secondhand fife to start practicing. That's precisely why this chapter includes deep insight into how to increase the longevity of your instrument and the aftercare and maintenance to keep it in perfect shape.

Fife Anatomy

The fife is a simple instrument with three basic parts: the mouthpiece, the body, and finger holes. Unlike the flute and piccolo, it only contains hollow finger holes and is a keyless system.

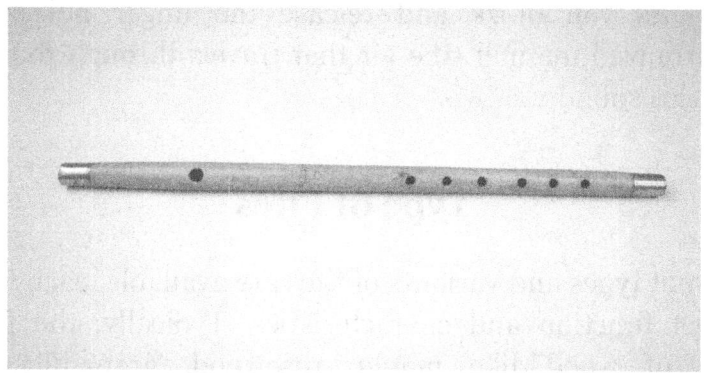

3. *The fife has three basic parts: the mouthpiece, the body, and finger holes. Source: Metropolitan Museum of Art, CC0, via Wikimedia Commons: https://commons.wikimedia.org/wiki/File:Fife_MET_midp1991.34 9.62.jpg*

The Mouthpiece

The mouthpiece is the main part of the fife where most of the action happens. This part is a small opening transporting the air into the fife's body. As the player blows air into the mouthpiece, it produces a sound.

The Body

The fife's body is a long and cylindrical tube and the central part of the instrument. Once the air is blown into the fife, the long conical pipe contains the internal mechanism to create sounds.

Finger Holes

The finger holes are evenly placed along the length of the instrument, varying in number depending on the fife. The basic fife has six finger holes, whereas other variants can contain 7, 10, and 11 holes. These small, hollow openings are the primary agents, allowing the player to create the pitch and notes. As you block and release the finger holes in a synchronized manner, the air that travels through the body produces sounds.

Type of Fifes

Different types and variants of fifes are available, each with a distinct function and characteristics. Typically, the fife is made of wood like maple, rosewood, granadilla, and blackwood. It is also available in metal and plastic bodies.

Standard Fife: The Basic Kind

Standard fife is the most common and basic type with six finger holes. This type is highly versatile and used primarily for military and marching bands. The standard fife is a good starter instrument for beginners and is made of wood or plastic.

Piccolo Fife: The Hybrid Kind

4. *The piccolo fife. Source: Dr. Nachtigaller, Public domain, via Wikimedia Commons:*
https://commons.wikimedia.org/wiki/File:Fasnachtspiccolo.jpg

The piccolo fife is a hybrid model typically smaller than the standard fife. This model contains higher finger holes and produces a higher pitch that is distinctly bright and shrill. The piccolo fifes add depth and penetrating quality to the music ensemble.

Plastic Fife: The Low-Maintenance Kind

The plastic fife is the perfect solution due to its sturdiness and affordability if you are a beginner. This variant is quite durable and resistant to temperature and humidity fluctuations. It is also great for use in educational and beginner music programs. This durable fife is perfect for outdoor performances, too.

Wood Fife: The Professional's Choice

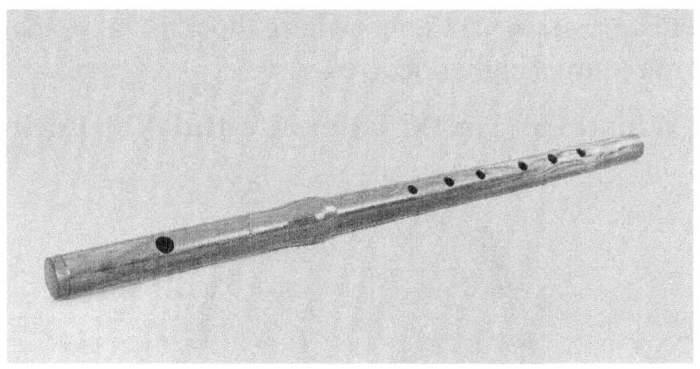

5. *Wood fife. Source: LB1918, GFDL <http://www.gnu.org/copyleft/fdl.html>, via Wikimedia Commons: https://commons.wikimedia.org/wiki/File:Schweizerpfeife_Fehr_ganz_2.jpg*

The wooden fife is perfect for a novice or intermediate fifer. Manufacturers use various woods, like maple and persimmon, to make high-quality fifes. The wood prominently influences the sound and produces a rich and warm tone in musical ensembles. Wooden fifes are mainly used to produce folk music and in historical reenactments.

Fife in F Key:

The F key fife is the most standard variant to play in the F key, mainly in the military context. It is used exclusively in ceremonial and military band performances. Based on the German naming system, this fife is named after the pitch it produces when played in C.

Key Mechanism Fife: The Advanced Kind

All major fifes are keyless systems, but there are always exceptions. This fife is quite advanced and used mainly in settings where the player must perform a broader range of notes than a standard one. You will mostly come across this fife in historical reenactments where the musical ensemble is rich and requires higher octaves.

Irish Whistle or Tin Whistle: Fife-But-Not-Entirely

6. *The Irish whistle isn't entirely classified as a fife. Source: Daniel Fernandez, CC BY-SA 3.0 <http://creativecommons.org/licenses/by-sa/3.0/>, via Wikimedia Commons: https://commons.wikimedia.org/wiki/File:Tin_Whistles.jpg*

Irish whistle isn't entirely classified as a fife since it has a narrow conical tube, but the haunting and distinctive sound it creates is quite similar to what the fife produces. Consider the tin whistle an off-shoot, a distant fife mostly used in Celtic and folk music.

Do not feel overwhelmed by the number of fife types out there. Getting acquainted with them allows aspiring players to pick one that suits their preferences, music context, and playing styles. The fife should align with your mastery level of the instrument. For instance, learning the ropes of fife, the standard fife, F fife, or a plastic one would be the right pick if you're a novice.

How to Maintain the Fife

Like any woodwind instrument, the fife requires proper care and maintenance to work properly. A well-kept, properly maintained fife is essential to producing a proper sound. Here's how you can extend the longevity of your instrument:

Proper Upkeep

You can't pull out your fife every time, belt out tunes, and tuck it back without proper upkeep. Whether a plastic fife or a wooden one, you must regularly clean the mouthpiece and wipe the interior with a swab using a cleaning rod. Cleaning at regular intervals ensures the fife stays and no residue is stuck in the mouthpiece. Remember, residual moisture is an enemy to this instrument.

Proper Storage Extends the Fife's Lifespan

How you store your fife after use is essential in extending the instrument's lifespan. Uneven and unnecessary exposure treme humidity and temperatures affect the sound and

- Keep the fife in a proper protective storage case to prevent dust accumulation.
- Make sure the protective case is lightly padded to avoid damaging the fife.

Periodic Inspection

Make it a habit to inspect your fife and identify issues or damages periodically. For instance, the common damages most fifes suffer are loose joints, body cracks, or damaged holes. A thorough inspection ensures you can address issues to the fife on time and avoid further damage.

Lubricate Wood Fifes

Wood fifes produce exceptionally warm, rich, and bright sounds. Professional fifers prefer them for their amazing tonal quality. However, they are prone to cracking when exposed to high temperatures or prolonged dryness. Make it a habit to apply bore oil to the interior at regular intervals to avoid this issue. It ensures the wood remains in prime condition and prevents crack formation.

Following these practices ensures your instrument is maintained in peak condition, allowing you to excel and master the fife without encountering problems.

Chapter 3: Decoding the Complex World of Fife Musical Notation

You're eager to start playing the fife. So, this chapter is one you don't want to overlook. Musical notation can be a source of frustration for many musicians and a daunting topic for beginners. Whether just starting out or gradually delving into the world of musical instruments, the biggest hurdle in your path might be familiarizing yourself with music theory. It's not as intimidating or complex as some people make it seem. This chapter provides the ultimate opportunity to become proficient in music notation and expedite your journey to mastering the fife.

Still Wondering Why Music Notation Is Essential for Fife Mastery?

7. *Learning musical notation can help you master an instrument. Source: https://pixabay.com/photos/music-notation-musical-melody-3207856/*

Mastering an instrument means you can create solid, coherent melodies, which isn't possible without knowing music reading skills. Similarly, to master the fife, you must understand the basic symbols and musical notations. The ability to decipher a standardized music sheet and the understanding of musical language will allow you to play any composition by following the transcription. Hence, the ability to decode and read musical transcription is sight reading. This guide will prepare you to understand sight reading in as little time as possible. You should put honest effort into understanding the information discussed in this chapter and follow through with the practical tips and exercises offered.

Decoding the Basics of Fife Music Sheet

The music sheet transcription is the art of transforming the ink into the sound. Once you understand all the symbols, you'll truly appreciate the magic of turning the notations into melodies.

Musical Staff — The Basic Canvas

The music staff is the foundation of every music sheet, denoted as five lines with four spaces. Since human ears can hear up to 20,000 notes, the five staff lines aren't enough for them all. Therefore, each line and space on the staff represents a note.

8. *Musical staff and clef. Source: https://pixabay.com/vectors/treble-clef-staff-notation-plain-304441/*

The Clef — Distinguish Pitches

The clef symbols distinguish the octave. These symbols are placed at the beginning of the staff to denote the note's pitch. The three clef types are treble, bass, and alto, and each indicates the varying pitch ranges.

Since the fife is played in a higher register, most of the music is written in the treble clef. It's also called G-clef,

ited by the symbol (□). The compositions written in
e clef indicate that the notes should be played in higher
......ical pitches. On the treble clefs, the notes are annotated with a pneumonic "FACE." Moreover, the note sequence travels up in alphabetical order from note A to G. The note sequence returns to A with a higher octave.

Decoding the Symbols — Notes, Rests, and Beyond

Notes — The Building Blocks of Melody

A note in musical notation is defined as a stylized notation that creates a melody when grouped together. In different variations, the musical notes denote its pitch and sound duration.

9. *Notes are the building blocks of melody. Source: https://pixabay.com/vectors/notes-music-music-notes-clef-1417670/*

In the same breath, you should know about 'accidentals.' These are instances where the notes are slightly adjusted and are sharp or flat. The sharp notes on a music sheet are notated with "#." The flat note is denoted with a "b" symbol, and both symbols are presented as a superscript. So, a B-flat is denoted as Bb, and a B-sharp is marked as B#.

Variation of Notes: The Rhythmic Values

Understanding the notes' rhythmic value is essential. They are based on various time divisions, so you must be familiar with whole, half, quarter, and eighth note duration to understand the composition's rhythmic quality.

The whole note is denoted with a hollow circle, informing the player to play the four complete beats. When you divide the music into two beats, it becomes a half-note, represented by a hollow circle and an attached stem. The filled circle symbol on the music sheet represents a quarter note, where the player has to play only one beat. Similarly, the eighth and sixteenth are again divided into two, and so on.

Whether you play whole and half notes or quarter and eighth notes, the sound produced remains the same, but the tempo varies in all instances. If you're wondering about 'tempo:' it's the speed of the musical composition, measured in beats per minute (bpm) and written in quarter notes.

Practice Drill to Improve Timing and Rhythm

As a beginner fifer, you need to develop a rhythmic quality. In this drill, you must clap along the different time duration rhythms to improve your sense of timing. The clapping exercise helps players develop rhythmic accuracy.

Understanding Rests: The Power of Silence

Notes are vital to the rhythm of music composition, but the even bigger superstar on the music sheet contributing to the dynamics and structure of an ensemble is called "rests." The rest is where you don't play the music, and note duration is where you play the composition. Like notes duration, rests also have whole, half, quarter, eighth, and sixteenth subdivisions.

10. Musical rest shapes. Source: Marmelad, Public domain, via Wikimedia Commons: https://commons.wikimedia.org/wiki/File:Music_rests.svg

First, the whole rest is like a hanging rectangle, similar to a musical pause button. It tells you to chill for four beats, like hitting pause on your favorite tune. Now, imagine a tiny hat sitting on the musical staff – that's the half rest. It's your cue to take a two-beat break. The quarter rest looks like a 'Z' and means a short pause for just one beat. Similar to catching a quick breath between musical moves. The eighth rest is a fancy 'R' in cursive. When you see it, stop the music for half a beat, like a musical pit stop. Lastly, the sixteenth rest is a swirly line with two flags. This one is a mini break for a quarter of a beat, like a short but sweet musical timeout. Let these symbols guide your fife-playing adventure and add groovy pauses to your fife composition. The most common rests and notes you will encounter when playing the fife are half notes.

Practice Drills to Understand Rests

The easiest way to understand and become acquainted with the rest is to count the duration out loud. This counting drill will ease you into becoming comfortable with smooth transitions and internalizing the rhythms.

Time Signatures

The time signature is a numerical representation signifying a music composition's count, which indicates the number of notes in a measure. The time signature is a fraction sign, like 2/4, ¾, 4/4, and 3/2. In these time signatures, the number on the top indicates the beat count, and the number on the bottom tells the player about the note (whole, half quarter, or so on) that must go with it. For instance, a 4/4 time signature requires the player to play four quarter notes in a single measure. The time signature is always located at the beginning of the staff unless there's a change in the composition.

Time Signatures Common with Fife

In music composition, the time signature primarily relies on the musical style and tradition. When learning the fife, it's good to be prepared about the time signatures you will encounter throughout the journey. Here are some common time signatures you'll find on fife music sheets.

2/4 Time Signature

This time signature is mostly in the marching band tunes to capture the fife's lively rhythmicity. In this time signature, you must play two-quarter notes in each bar.

6/8 Time Signature

This particular time signature is mostly found in various folk and traditional music pieces with a sense of vibrancy and playfulness. The 6/8 time signature is also linked to the jigs genre, as it imbues the tunes with a rhythmic quality. This time signature features six eighth notes per bar.

2/2 Time Signature

Also known as cut time, you must play two half notes per beat in a recurring pattern in this time signature. This time signature is commonly found in music compositions with higher energy and faster momentum.

4/4 Time Signature

This time signature can also be denoted with a 'C' on the music sheet, known as common time. It might not be popular in many genres but is frequently played in fife music. It adds a steady rhythm to the fife tunes.

3/4 Time Signature

11. ¾ time signature example. Source: Wereon, Public domain, via Wikimedia Commons: https://commons.wikimedia.org/wiki/File:Time_signature_example.svg

This time signature isn't too widely used in the fife music, but you'll occasionally encounter it. It requires playing three-quarter notes in one measure, adding a waltz feel to the composition and giving it a steady structure and rhythmic quality.

Key Signatures

Key notations indicate the scale of the composition they are meant to be played in. You'll find the key right behind the time signature at the beginning of a staff.

A scale is a sequence of notes played together. In the next chapter, you'll learn how to play various notes on the fife that ultimately plays like a scale. So, coming back to key signatures, most of the tonal music is played in a major or minor scale following the same pattern with a slight change at the starting point. For instance, the C major scale and the A minor scale have the same notes but are phrased differently. Similarly, the common scales you'll encounter in fife music are D major, G major, and A major.

How to Read and Interpret Simple Melodies for Fife

You have now become acquainted with the essential notation on a music sheet. They won't seem like incoherent and senseless symbols anymore. Now's the time to move on to the next step.

Sight Reading

Regular sight reading is an essential skill for every aspiring musician. It involves playing a piece by following the notation sheet without rehearsal. Once you begin, sight reading will take considerably more effort, but as you gradually expose yourself to various music compositions, you'll become more adept. This skill allows the musician to adapt to any music style and play the compositions more easily. For beginner fifers, it's essential to invest time in sight reading, follow easy melodies initially, and eventually graduate to more complex tunes.

Get into the Groove: Start with Familiar Tones

Getting better at interpreting the music requires players to expose themselves to music notation sheets. Find familiar tunes, like "Twinkle, Twinkle, Little Star" or other easy tunes, and download its music notation sheet. Reinforce everything you've learned in this chapter, decode what each notation and symbol stands for, and practice. This drill helps you become comfortable with music reading, and interpreting the sheet won't seem like an alien thing anymore.

Common Challenges Fifers Face with Music Notation Sheets and How to Overcome Them

Learning how to read music can be overwhelming for beginners, but the right foundations will lay the most groundwork. This section addresses the most common challenges and issues beginners face with music sheets.

Problem: The Music Sheet Is Too Complex, I Can't Crack It

As a beginner learning to play, there will be times when faced with a seemingly incomprehensible music sheet. Some sheets can be overwhelming with tempo variances and keys.

Solution: Take It Slow and Opt for Segmented Practice

The solution is to stay level-headed. Whenever you have a challenging or complex music sheet, break it down into manageable, smaller sections. Also, there's no need to practice the broken sections in the same tempo from the first go. Start practicing at a slow pace several times until you are comfortable picking up the tempo. Moreover, if even breaking down into sections seems complicated, you can further divide the composition into small phrases and master them before playing the whole piece in one go.

The golden rule is to divide, practice, and conquer the composition.

Problem: I Can't Match the Tempo of the Composition

Many novices lose their motivation to play a composition if they can't match the tempo. Don't set your expectations too high from the get-go. Even professional players cannot match the composition tempo every time. It takes practice.

Solution: Get a Metronome — Your Rhythmic Ally

12. *A metronome can help you maintain a steady tempo. Source: https://unsplash.com/photos/white-printer-paper-on-brown-wooden-table-EjmcT09e3Jg?utm_content=creditShareLink&utm_medium=referral&utm_source=unsplash*

First and foremost, whenever you have a music sheet in front of you, practice slowly and forget about the tempo. Once you master a particular section, raise the tempo gradually. But this is only the tip of the iceberg.

The real solution to your problem is a metronome. It's a valuable tool allowing the player to maintain a steady tempo. Once you get the hang of the music composition, practicing with a metronome is always advisable, as it improves the rhythm and timing. Moreover, it adds precision to your playing. To practice, try tapping some rhythms with a metronome. Stay consistent, and your tempo will improve.

Once you invest time in understanding music notation, the rest of the fife learning journey will be a breeze.

Chapter 4: The Secrets of Mastering Proper Fingering Techniques

The first step toward mastering the art of playing fife is learning how to get a good hold of it and practicing the correct posture. This chapter introduces you to the right finger placements on your fife and bombards you with fingering exercises to master the skill.

Learn How to Hold the Fife

The fife is a sideways-played woodwind instrument. It should be held on the right side of the face, perfectly parallel to the ground. Hold your fife up to your mouth using both hands, ensuring your left hand is placed close to your face and the right hand toward the end of the fife. Your left hand's palm should face your mouth, while your left hand's palm should face away from your mouth.

13. Learning to hold the fife correctly can make a huge difference in sound. Source: https://pixabay.com/photos/fife-tambourine-storyteller-2700890/

Now, your next goal is to work up the six holes on your right.

The fingers for sound production and manipulation of the fife are the index, middle, and ring fingers on both hands. Put your hands before you and number your fingers for easy learning. Your index finger on the left hand is the first, your middle finger is the second, and the ring finger is the third. Similarly, number your right-hand fingers 4, 5, and 6, moving from the index finger to the ring finger. Now, you can practice holding up your fife with the designated fingers placed on their respective keyholes. When you hold the fife right, your palms will face the correct direction automatically.

If you're holding it right, you must have figured out the role of your thumbs and pinkies. They support the body of the fife and build the correct pressure on it while you play. Placing your thumbs and pinky fingers on the fife is quite an intuitive process, and you can do it as you feel comfortable. However, some fife professionals place their thumb on the fife directly below their index finger to secure it firmly. On the other hand, the pinkies are made to rest on the fife's top surface to build downward pressure in effortless balance with the thumb. This dynamic of the thumbs and pinkies controls your fife holding as it eases the fingering mechanics and keeps your fife straight and stable throughout the practice.

Get a Little Hands-On

You now have a fife in your hand and know the correct finger placement. In the next section, you'll learn to play the C major scale. The C-major scale is where all fife players build their fife playing foundation. Since this is your first try at fingering a scale, focus on holding your fife steady and try to transition through the notes seamlessly.

The C-major scales are C-D-E-F-G-A-B-C. It is a standard, and you must learn it by heart like all other scales. Now, put your fife to your mouth and blow into it following the steps below.

- **Play a C:** Keep your fingers covering all six holes as you blow. The sound you hear is how the lowest note on a fife sounds.

- **Play a D:** Keep blowing into the fife steadily, and lift your index finger from the first hole as light as a feather. Put your finger down again softly to end the note.

- **Play an E**: Lift your middle finger from the second hole.

- **Play an F**: Lift your ring finger from the third hole, and you have produced an F note.
- You will notice a pattern break here: pay attention.
- **Play a G:** Lift your ring finger from the sixth hole to produce the G note.
- **Play an A:** To produce the A note, lift your right index finger from the fourth hole.
- **Play a B:** To produce the B note, lift your right middle finger from the fifth hole.
- **Play a C again**: Cover all the six holes with your six playing fingers, and you have a C note—this time, you have to hit the C note at its highest. Everything remains the same. You only have to blow a little forcefully starting with this transition.

A few things to remember: after each note, place your finger down gently. The transition between notes happens in this lifting up and down of the fingers. Moving your fingers on the keyholes like soft dabs when playing fife is vital, as it contributes to the notes' finesse.

Although you are supposed to transition between the notes with light fingers, it doesn't mean you should leave the keyholes half open. The keyholes must be covered fully so the air only escapes from the keyhole you are playing to produce the best fife sounds. Also, when you uncover a keyhole to play a particular note, lift the finger at a maximal distance so it doesn't hover over the key or get in the way of the air's outflow.

Specific Fingering Techniques

As a beginner, put in extra time and effort to master the notes from the above. The art of fife-playing lies in a smooth transition, quality sound production, and seamless alternating finger movements.

The first half of the song below has the notes C-C-G-G-A-A-G. You know how to play these notes from earlier. Try to play them from your memory, and check with the instructions below if you got the keys right.

Fingering Instructions of "Twinkle, Twinkle Little Star"

- Play the lowest C note by gently blowing into the fife while covering all keyholes. This note corresponds to "twinkle."

- Play another lowest C note the same way. It will correspond to the second twinkle.

- Play the G note by lifting your finger from the first hole while gently blowing into the fife. This note plays the "lit" in the little.

- Play another G note without closing the keyhole in between. You are still playing the same "lit."

- Play an A note by lifting your middle finger from the second hole. This note will play the "tle" in the little.

- Play the second A note by lifting your finger as you did earlier while playing "lit." You will keep the second hole uncovered throughout.

- Return your middle finger to the second hole. Now, you will play the final G note by lifting your ring finger from the sixth hole.

You have now played your first song on the fife. Are you looking for more fingering practice? It's time you practice the notes to the second phrase, "How I wonder what you are," on your own: F-F-E-E-D-D-C.

Basics to Keep in Mind

People often jump into playing the instrument without training their fingers properly. Another thing that gets overlooked by fife players is their posture.

Finger Dexterity Practices

Strengthening your fingers through various exercises will help you practice for hours without wearing out. These exercises allow you to play expressive music with great precision and control.

- **Squeeze, Squeeze**

Take a soft cotton or rubber ball and repeatedly squeeze and release it. This exercise will tone your finger muscles and help you apply controlled pressure using your finger pads.

- **Finger Stretch**

Hold your palms in the air, and stretch your fingers apart as much as possible. Hold the position for a few seconds, then relax your fingers. This stretch will make your fingers flexible over time.

- **Finger Climbing**

Imagine your fingers are climbing a staircase. Begin lifting your fingers one by one, starting from the index finger, then bring them down in reverse. These finger movements will train them to switch between notes.

- **Note the Correct Fife Posture**

The best posture for playing the fife is the player's feet planted on the floor, and their hands rested at 90 degrees. You can use a music stand or practice sitting on a chair. Having well-rested hands prevents you from getting tired too early. The second most crucial postural consideration for fifers is relaxed shoulders and a straight back. Keeping a straight back while playing helps the player inhale and exhale deeply, directly impacting the sound quality produced.

With these basics in mind, practice the finger drills and postural setting before you pick up the fife the next time.

Chapter 5: Producing Your First Tones

In the previous chapter, you mastered the fingering movement on fife and learned to play different notes and songs. Now, it's time to learn how to create perfect sounds on the fife. A lot of skillful manipulation of embouchure and breath control go into producing fine-tuned sounds.

Sound Production

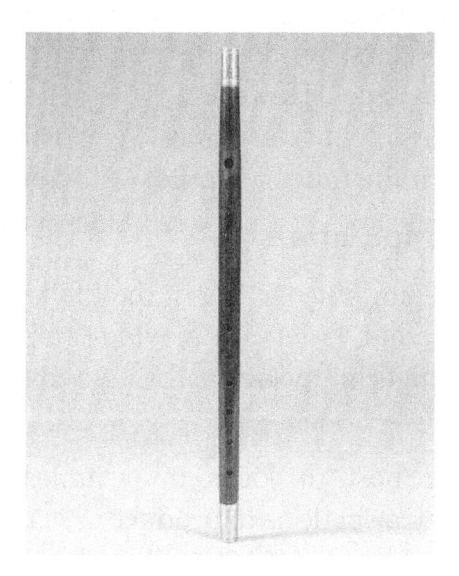

14. The fife produces sounds by the vibration of air particles moving inside its hollow bore. Source: Metropolitan Museum of Art, CC0, via Wikimedia Commons: https://commons.wikimedia.org/wiki/File:Fife_MET_DT8479.jpg

Like all woodwind instruments, the fife also produces sounds by the vibration of air particles moving inside its hollow bore. But there's more to sound production than simply blowing air into the fife.

Dynamics of Air Column

The straight and long air column is where sound production happens. A player blows into the fife with a constant air seam that travels through its body, creating waves. The turbulence and the hitting of these waves against the walls make sounds when they reach the other end.

The Sound Hole

Like a flute, the fife has a sound hole in the mouthpiece. A fifer can do wonders by blowing into the sound hole with different mouth shapes. However, the experts keep a tight lip throughout their fife performance. You will learn how to produce different fife tones with the perfect embouchure.

Fingering Manipulation

The covering and uncovering of the fife keyholes shift the flow of the air stream. Practicing playing the fife will teach you how different fingering positions bring about change in the fife sounds.

It would be best to focus on seamless blowing and articulated fingering actions to produce a clear and consistent tone from a fife. Initially, it looks like a lot of work, but it is only a matter of time until you build muscle memory to the primary breath control and fingering motions.

Learning Proper Embouchure

The embouchure refers to shaping the mouth and positioning the lips on the mouthpiece. You must have seen different woodwind instrument players holding their instrument on their lower lip as they blow into it with puckered lips. That's what the correct embouchure looks like. Here's a breakdown of the proper embouchure:

- **Placement of the Lips:** Bring your fife close to your mouth and place it on the lower margin of your bottom lip. Make sure the sound hole lies on top uncovered and is aligned with the center of your philtrum (the midline groove in the upper lip). You can practice holding the fife on your lips several times until you find the best spot to rest it.

- **Shaping of the Lip**: You already have your fife propped up against your lower lip. It's time you pucker up your upper lip and make it hover over the sound hole. In this position, if you blow into the sound hole, you'll hear a sweet fife sound pour out of the other end. This puckered lip position is cardinal because it directs the airflow straight into the sound hole at the right angle and pressure.

- **Tonguing:** Imagine your tongue as a lid that opens and closes your mouth over the sound hole. To blow into the fife, first remove your tongue from your mouth opening and place it behind the front two teeth. This way, you'll start your blowing with a slight "tho" sound every time. Similarly, you end your note by placing your tongue back on the opening of your mouth.

Making the perfect embouchure takes a lot of practice and patience. It makes or breaks the fifer's performance, as it directly impacts the quality and pitch of the sound produced.

You already know how to hold the fife and shape your lips for an embouchure. But there's a bit more you need to know. Have you wondered how wide you should open your mouth for the proper embouchure? Yes, you're supposed to have tight lips throughout the blowing process, with your lips opening only the size of a crack. This precise opening of the lips gives you a precision-led embouchure where the sound quality is entirely in your control.

Here's an easy embouchure practice to help you understand the right amount of parting between your lips. Place a dry rice between your lips, and blow out until the rice pops out. That's how much you are supposed to part your lips. It might appear daunting initially, but you'll get the hang of it with practice.

Breath Control Exercises to Develop Steady Airflow

To begin breath control practice, start with diaphragmatic breathing. A fifer needs to inhale profoundly using their diaphragm. It's not their chest that heaves but their abdomen that moves in and out.

15. Practicing breath control will help you play the fife better. Source: https://www.pexels.com/photo/woman-in-white-crew-neck-t-shirt-holding-black-flute-4709857/

Once you have the hang of the diaphragmatic breath, it's time to delve into some fife exercises.

Exercise 1: Play Long Notes

In the previous chapter, you learned to play different notes on the fife. This time, play those same notes but with your focus on playing them for as long as possible. Bring all your attention to keeping a persistent airflow into the fife so that the sound has an even tone throughout.

It would be best to practice blowing your fife with all six holes closed and experimenting with different fingering patterns. Pick up any notes from the previous chapter and play them on your fife for an extended duration. This drill is not to test your finger dexterity but to help you get command over seamless airflow and stable fife sounds.

Exercise 2: Articulation

An excellent fifer knows how to initiate and end the note clearly and with defined demarcation. Making each note you play on the fife sound distinct and clear without breaking the melody is a deft process. This is where your tongue comes in. Practicing articulation in fife playing is like starting each note with a tap from your tongue.

- **Try Playing Staccato:** The staccato notes are short and bouncy notes to bring an exciting factor to the fife melody. Playing a staccato is a game of swift and rapid articulation. With these notes, fifers move their tongue back and forth from their mouth, like "tu-tu-tu" to add the bouncy effect.

- **Try Playing Legato:** Legato is the opposite of staccato. It involves a lot of articulations, but here, your tongue joins the notes together. While playing, your tongue remains relaxed and swiftly slips back up by the tune's end. The legato plays out on the fife like a long note that continues like a single "Laaa."

Exercise 3: Dynamics

A tune's dynamics is the range of how loud or soft you play it. The fife has a range of two octaves. So, you can easily play your notes two octaves higher or lower. Producing a softer and louder sound on the same notes is solely the work of embouchure. Every fife player should master this early because playing between the octaves increases your performance's liveness. Remember, a good fife performance is well-played and expressive at the same time.

- **Practice Crescendo:** To play a crescendo, start a note with slow blowing and then escalate it to a louder pitch. You don't need to make any alterations to the fingering here. It's best to swiftly escalate the pressure of the air you blow into the bore.

- **Practice Decrescendo:** In a decrescendo, you bring the melody down to a softer pitch from the louder one. You play a decrescendo by starting at a higher pitch and then slowly making the sound softer by decreasing the pressure you blow into the bore.

Exercise 4: Vibrato

Practicing vibrato will be the most difficult of these four exercises. But to be a skilled fifer, you must dabble in every practice added to the history of fife. Unlike the other exercises in vibrato, your fingers will work in unison with your embouchure. Here's how you bring an emotional depth to the fife melody using vibrato.

- **Practice Wobbling:** To create a vibrato effect on a particular note, wobble your finger over the keyhole involved. Like repeatedly covering and uncovering the same hole with a shaking motion.

- **Play with the Pitch**: The alterations in the pitch are partly brought about by the finger motion, but you must also make precise changes to the embouchure. Keep your tongue relaxed throughout, and loosen your lips quickly to shift the blowing pressure.

Mastering the different ways of playing the fife takes time. All you need to do is adapt well to the anatomy of the fife and play it by understanding its physical dynamics. As a novice, you only need to get competent at playing notes and jumping between octaves. It is only a matter of time until you advance your repertoire by leaps and master complex melodies.

Chapter 6: Basic Melodies and Exercises

By now, if you've been practicing while going through the chapters and following the detailed instructions, practice materials, and drills, you've undoubtedly grown accustomed to playing the fife. Congratulations, you might not be a master at the fife just yet, but you can still churn out smooth notes and scales. This chapter is the next big step on your fife learning journey.

Warm Up for the Next Big Leap

At this point, you know your way around the fife. You have correct posture, proper fingering technique, and developed a solid embouchure. Now you're ready to amp up your fife skills. This section puts your fife beginner-level skills to practical use. Learn how you can belt out melodies with the fife like a pro.

Ace the Tempo

Acing the fife is natural and easy, and the tune structure comprises a solo melody line paired with a percussive drum line. The fife melodies do not include additional harmonization. Therefore, maintaining the tempo is a high priority. One way to maintain it is to follow the metronome.

16. A fife is widely used as a marching instrument. Source: https://pixabay.com/photos/appomattox-fife-civil-war-battle-1178538/

But there's another interesting way to match the tempo. As you know, fife is widely used as a marching instrument. It was also a great way to match the tune's tempo with the marching pattern. In this practice, a player matches their marching steps with the note value. For instance, if the time signature is 4/4, the player will march with the right foot on 1 and 3 bars and the left foot on 2 and 4 of 4/4 bars.

If you're interested in playing the fife in a marching band, this practice is the perfect way to nail the tempo. If you're running out of breath or losing posture, give up marching. Instead, you can opt for the foot-tapping technique on 1,2,3,4.

Build Mastery Over Long Notes

Before getting in the groove to play complex tunes and renditions, you must warm up your fingers. The best exercise for this is playing long, steady, and consistent notes. You can begin by practicing with four consecutive whole notes at a steady tempo.

Get Groovy with the Scales

The three major scales you should learn to play with the fife are D, G, and A. These three scales are quite similar, saving you from excessive memorization. For instance, the G major scale has F#, D-major has F# and C#, and A-major has F#, C#, and G# notes. Once you learn to play the scales, you'll be ready to unleash the fife melodies quickly.

Tips to Master the Scales — Fast and Easy

Before you learn to play these scales, here are some essential tips:

- Each scale has a group of notes, and to ensure steady and consistent playing, memorize the fingerings for each note first. It also helps you avoid looking back and forth to the music sheet.

- A common mistake many fife players must correct is the wrong fingering. Some players do not lift their fingers off during notes transition properly. Move the fingers with proper dexterity and lift them completely for a clean sound.

- When playing the scales, switch between note dynamics. Play some notes softer and others louder to add more color and expression to the tunes.

How to Play A-Major Scale

The note composition for the A-major scale is A, B, C#, D, E, F#, G#, and A. When you prepare to play the scale, maintain a relaxed and easy finger posture with natural curvature to avoid stiffness when moving between the notes. While you follow the fingering to move through the notes, the thumb should be placed against the fife's body to keep it stable. Make sure that your thumb does not block or press against the holes.

- To play A, place your 1st and 2nd fingers over the two holes and blow the air in the mouthpiece.

- Put your index finger over the first hole to play the B note and blow into the fife.

- For the next note in the sequence, lift your fingers from all the holes and allow the free flow of air to get C#. This note is all about the correct and steady embouchure.

- To play D, gradually place the index, middle, and ring fingers on holes 1, 2, and 3.

- The final note to play is E. Cover all four holes with three fingers from the right hand and the pinky finger on the fourth hole, and continue to play the rest of the notes.

How to Play D Major Scale

The note sequence of the D-major scale is D, E, F#, G, and A. Follow and memorize the fingering position for each note to play the scale.

Free Jamming

Follow the music sheets and practice with the composition. But there's another effective way to get better at playing the fife. All you have to do is get your fife out and play the notes without following any written composition. Jamming sessions allow you to tweak and improvise your notes, helping you improve expression and phrasing. This allows you to improve your techniques and develop a good ear.

How to Get Comfortable Playing Songs on Fife

To improve faster, it's best to practice with the songs. Before you start playing the tune, make sure you know the time signature, scale, and tempo in addition to figuring out the rhythm. Once you've figured out all the essentials, follow the music chart and fingerings. Try to play "Ode To Joy" and "The Saints Go Marching In" on the first.

A Helpful Tutorial to Play "Ode To Joy"

"Ode to Joy" is a popular tune known for its joyful expression. This tune is played in a D major scale with two sharp notes, F#, and C#, in a 4/4 time signature. Throughout the composition, you'll find a combination of whole, half, quarter, and eighth notes. Hop on to the previous chapters for a reminder on how to play these notes if necessary. This tune is played at 140 bpm.

To play this tune on a Bb fife, follow the scale: D, E, F#, G, A, B, C#, D. On a 6-hole Bb fife, you will play the following notes, Bb, C, D, E, F, G, A. Familiarize yourself with fingering for this piece and break down the composition into smaller sections. Experiment with the dynamics to add tonality to your practice when playing the tune.

A Helpful Tutorial to Play "The Saints Go Marching In"

Here's another popular folk tune to practice on the fife. You can practice this tune on any fife model. This tutorial will give insight on how to play the tune on a 7-hole fife. The composition is in F major scale.

- Maintain a steady posture, hold your fife correctly, and create a strong and tight embouchure.
- Warm up and produce the right sound.
- The first phrase for this tune is C, E, F, G.
- Set the embouchure on the mouthpiece, cover all 7 holes with fingers 1-7, and blow air to create a steady sound to play note C.
- Similarly, cover holes 1-5 with fingers 1-5 and blow the air, then cover four holes with the four fingers the same way to create the notes E and F.
- Then, cover holes 1, 2, and 3 with the fingers 1, 2, 3, and blow air to create a sound for note G.
- The next phrase will be C, E, F, G, E, C, E, D.
- Cover holes 1-7 with the fingers to play C and blow once.

- Then, cover the 5 holes with the right finger position and blow again to get an E.
- Next, to play an F, cover the four holes and blow the air.
- Cover the three holes with the index, middle, and ring finger to play G.
- Then, follow the same fingering position to play the notes E, C, E as above.
- To play note D, cover the six holes with both hands' index, middle, and ring finger.
- You have the two major phrases of this tune. Now, practice the notes once more. Then, steadily play both phrases to produce a smooth melody.
- The third phrase for "The Saints Go Marching In" is E, D, C, C, E, G, G, F.
- For this phrase, follow the fingering patterns given in the above steps.
- The next phrase for this tune is E, F, G, E, C, D, C. Follow the fingering for each note.
- Once you have practiced all the phrases, play the entire tune. Depending on how soft or loud you blow into the mouthpiece, you can experiment with the pitch.

This chapter was packed with lessons on amplifying your fife skills with instructions to play complete melodies. You'll feel highly confident in your fife skills by following through with the practical drills offered in this chapter.

Chapter 7: Exploring Different Musical Styles and Level Up Fife Skills with Intermediate Techniques and Genre Exploration

Any instrument, not only fife, offers endless possibilities once you jump through the hoops of beginner-level skills. Once you get past the fingering basics, posture issues, and getting the embouchure right, you'll wonder what's next. There's a bigger world of fife out there. This chapter is all about what's next. It's time to get serious and explore the instrument's application in various genres and a few intermediate techniques that will make you stand out from the crowd of mediocre fifers.

Learn Advanced Fife Techniques

You now know the basics of playing the fife. It's time to add your personal touch to your compositions and improve your skills. The intermediate techniques like legato, trills, and dynamics add more expression and personality to your fife-playing skills.

Get Acquainted with Triplets

Fife has simple melodies and rhythms, but it isn't always easy. You can also get more ambitious and complex with rhythmic variants. The triplet is the rhythmic value of a note divided into three parts. However, it is quite challenging for musicians to count and maintain the tempo of the note in triplets. In intermediate music compositions, you'll often find triplets. To nail them, simultaneously tap the left and right hand on the beat note.

Add Depth with Trills

The trill is a great intermediate technique where the alternating notes are played in quick succession. The trill is denoted with 'tr' on the music sheet. This technique isn't dependent on the breathing technique. Instead, it is the swift-fingering action to block and unblock the holes for specific notes in a smooth transition.

Play with Chromatic Fingering

The chromatic notes imply that it includes seven or eleven-note degrees. According to the standardized western division of frequencies, the 11 notes are called chromatic scales. The fife plays the chromatic notes within three octaves.

Try and Play with Octave Variances

The change in the mouthpiece's breathing angle allows the player to produce low and high notes. You must modify the breathing technique to achieve higher octaves on the fife.

Effective Breathing Drill

Place your hands on your belly and breathe from the diaphragm. As you breathe, let out a deep tone that should come out as 'ha-Ah.' When you're practicing this drill, you'll notice the amount of breath you exhale will be the same, but the firmness in your belly indicates you're breathing from the diaphragm, not from the throat.

Effective Drill for Higher Notes

The secret to producing high notes and octaves is an open, clear throat or windpipe. Moreover, keep a tight embouchure by controlling it via the center of the mouth. When you focus on the philtrum muscle for embouchure, you can blow the air for higher octaves.

Explore Fife in Various Genres

When you become adept at playing the fife, consider exploring various common genres for this instrument.

17. The fife can be played in many different genres. Source: https://www.pexels.com/photo/retro-cassette-records-in-stacks-15447298/

Folk and Traditional Music

Fife is the heartbeat of folk and traditional tunes. You'll find culturally significant tunes passed down from generation to generation. Combining fife and drums creates a stunning impact on contemporary folk music.

Baroque and Classical Music

Classic and baroque tunes provide an expressive and immersive experience to the listeners. You can utilize fife to practice rich and classic compositions, elevating your status to produce highly dynamic sounds.

Historical Reenactments

Fifes are the first choice of instrument in historical reenactment performances. Many fifers in the military and performance bands use the instrument to create sounds and tunes of the American Civil War and Revolutionary War. You can also use one of these music repertoires to refine your skills.

Contemporary Music

While fife sounds great for folk tunes, there's no reason you shouldn't experiment with modern and contemporary tunes. Select your favorite pop hits and adapt them to play with the fife.

Cross Genre Fusion

Experimentation with various music styles adds a sense of freedom and confidence in the musician's instrument skills. Blending elements from different genres is always a great idea to add a nuanced and distinct flavor to your compositions. So, don't be afraid of testing your limits with cross-genre fusions.

Exploring varied music styles and adding intermediate techniques to your fife-playing sessions further exposes you to the instrument's intricacies.

Chapter 8: Progressing as a Fife Player

Congratulations on reaching the last leg of your fife mastery journey. Following the insightful path carved in this book has all the targeted and practical strategies to make you the novice fifer you always wanted to become. While you've mastered the fife basics and can call yourself a fifer, the journey is far from finished.

How to Progress From a Beginner to a Pro

Set Clear Musical Goals

18. Setting clear goals can help you progress as a fife player. Source: https://www.pexels.com/photo/white-earphones-near-papers-269610/

Learning the instrument effectively and sustainably requires setting achievable and clear objectives. Make a list of your strong and weak areas. Prepare a checklist of the goals you want to achieve, i.e., mastering the embouchure, decoding a challenging tune, or learning new and advanced techniques in a specific genre.

Don't Set Extremely High Expectations

You can't plan to master the fife in a week and start playing with professional musicians and bands. This is unrealistic. You should always plan small milestones in your fife learning journey.

Develop Proper Ear Training

Expose yourself to fife compositions and develop a repertoire. Listen to various music styles, genres, and complexities to train your ears. Listening to music compositions allows you to understand what sounds right and what doesn't.

Record Yourself Playing

Whenever you play different tunes and melodies, record yourself and listen to them. Listening to your recordings will help you assess and identify areas for improvement.

Regular Practice Shouldn't Take a Backseat

Regular fife practice sessions are the ultimate solution to improving your skills. Extensive practice sessions ensure you don't lose what you learned.

Participate in a Performance Ensemble

If you wish to develop confidence and mastery over the fife, practicing with an ensemble or a performance band is the best way. Playing with musicians at the same skill level as you or above will help you improve your tonality and rhythm.

Never Run Out of Melodies to Practice Fife

Many novice players often find it challenging to find tunes to practice with. To add a few great tunes to your practice repertoire, here are some great picks to get you started, helping you build up to more challenging tunes.

- **Yankee Doodle:** This American melody symbolized patriotism during the American Revolutionary War.

- **The Minstrel Boy:** This Irish song featuring the fife conveys resilience and heroism. This melody is often played with drums.
- **Gary Owens:** This popular military tune has a great fife presence and represents the American Civil War Era.
- **The Girl I Left Behind Me:** Fife had a significant appearance in European folk tunes. This Irish and British traditional tune features fife in various arrangements mostly played during marching and military performances.
- **Iconic Fife and Drum:** No fife repertoire would be complete without adding a fife and drum composition.

Immerse Yourself in the World of Fife

Like with any instrument, mastery comes from constant exposure. Immerse yourself in the rich and historical tapestry of the fife. To become a master fifer, you must allow it to inspire you. What's better than finding inspiration from legendary musicians? Here are the top five picks of popular fifers you should explore.

- Alfred 'Snappy' Nappy contributed greatly to the fife's popularity by incorporating it into jazz and contemporary music. Explore his work and identify how his fife skills earned him stardom in gospel music.
- Bruce Hutton is a well-known fifer in the American military music sphere. He was a prominent

member of fifers and drummers aimed at preserving the fife and drum music art.

- Cotton Bailey was a renowned fife educator and performer. He is also responsible for keeping this instrument alive and intriguing for the new generation of aspiring fifers. As a novice fifer, you should explore his compositions in the traditional American fife and drum company.

- Mark L. Gardener highlighted military music of the Civil War era and is well-known for performing historical music performances.

- Luis Garcia Sanz stands out in the list of contemporary fife players. He is well-known for using the fife in Spanish music. So, if you're interested in learning how to incorporate fife in Spanish music along with contemporary influence, you should definitely check out his work.

You've finally reached the end of this book, but remember, the journey to fife mastery is long and exciting. It's a continuous adventure, so be ambitious and maintain your excitement. Remember, the musical progression is all about expressing and evolving into this resonance and rhythm-filled journey with the fife.

Conclusion

In this comprehensive exploration, you delved into the multifaceted world of the fife, unraveling its unique charm and musical intricacies. Your journey began with an introductory overview, laying the groundwork for a profound understanding of this often-overlooked instrument and its historical significance.

You acquainted yourself with the essence of the fife, drawing distinctions between it and its musical counterparts, the piccolo and the flute. By discerning the nuanced differences in structure and musical role, you established a solid foundation for your journey.

With practicality in mind, you navigated the practical aspects of fifes. You explored the anatomy of the instrument and received essential insight into the various fifes available. Additionally, you obtained valuable maintenance tips and tricks, ensuring the longevity of this delicate instrument.

The intricacies of fife musical notation unfolded in your subsequent segment. Your journey through this chapter involved a comprehensive examination of the musical staff, clefs, notes, rests, and more. Armed with this knowledge, you are prepared to read and interpret simple melodies while enhancing your sight-reading proficiency. You also addressed common challenges encountered by fifers and presented effective solutions to surmount them, empowering yourself to conquer even the most complex musical sheets.

Your progress continued as you examined the secrets of mastering precise fingering techniques. From learning how to hold the fife correctly to practicing specific fingering techniques, you equipped yourself with the skills necessary for playing the fife with precision and grace.

The journey pressed on as you ventured into the domain of sound production on the fife. You explored the mechanics of the air column, understood the significance of the sound hole, and learned to manipulate fingering to produce resonant tones. Furthermore, you shared insights into breath control exercises and developed embouchure techniques to refine sound production.

This exploration transitioned to the realm of playing basic melodies and exercises. You were encouraged to warm up, refine your tempo, and master long notes. Scales, like the A major and D minor scales, were introduced as fundamental building blocks, enabling the pursuit of more intricate musical endeavors.

Stepping up to the next level of proficiency, you explored various musical styles and introduced intermediate techniques. You became acquainted with concepts such as triplets, trills, chromatic fingering, and octave variances, enabling you to infuse depth and complexity into your playing. Effective drills for tackling higher notes were presented, preparing you to explore a broader spectrum of musical genres.

Lastly, you were encouraged to pursue continuous progress and discovered how to maintain enthusiasm by never running out of melodies to practice. Immersion into the world of the fife was celebrated, inviting you to explore and experiment with your newly acquired skills.

The fife is not merely a historical artifact. It is a living, breathing component of the musical landscape. Whether you aspire to be a proficient performer or simply wish to savor the joys of playing, the knowledge and skills you acquired through this exploration provide the key to unlocking the boundless potential of the fife. The world of the fife is open for discovery and enjoyment, and with each note played, you contribute to its enduring legacy.

References

Fife (musical instrument). (n.d.). Academic Dictionaries and Encyclopedias. https://en-academic.com/dic.nsf/enwiki/265939

Randall, J. (2022). How to Play the Fife: A Beginner's Guide to Learning the Basics, Reading Music, and Playing Songs with Audio Recordings (Woodwinds for Beginners). Independently Published.

wikiHow. (2008, July 28). 3 Ways to Play the Fife. WikiHow. https://www.wikihow.com/Play-the-Fife

Made in United States
North Haven, CT
12 September 2025